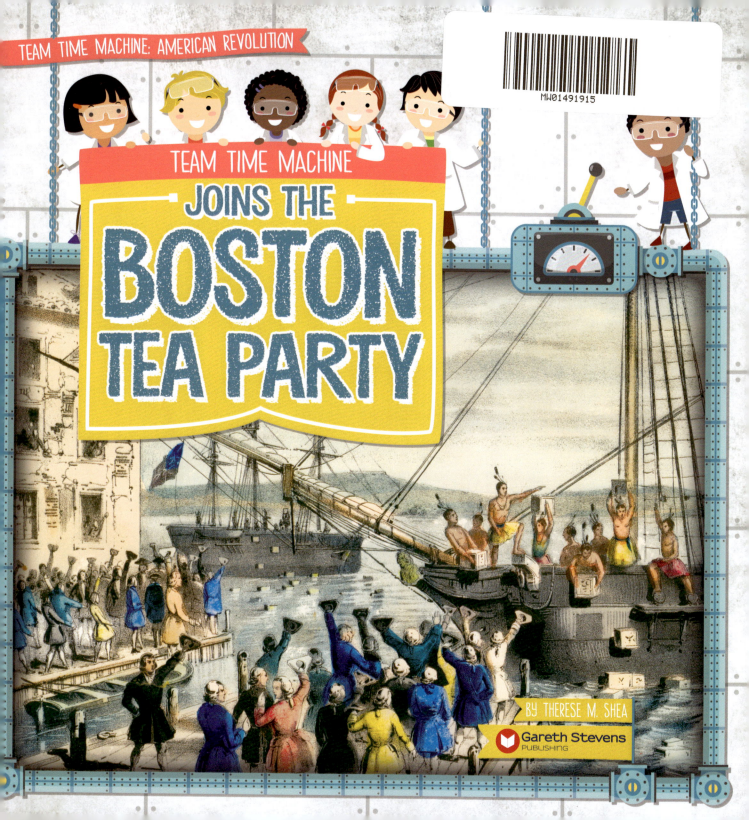

TEAM TIME MACHINE: AMERICAN REVOLUTION

TEAM TIME MACHINE
JOINS THE
BOSTON
TEA PARTY

BY THERESE M. SHEA

Gareth Stevens
PUBLISHING

Please visit our website, www.garethstevens.com. For a free color catalog of all our high-quality books, call toll free 1-800-542-2595 or fax 1-877-542-2596.

Library of Congress Cataloging-in-Publication Data

Names: Shea, Therese, author.
Title: Team Time Machine Joins the Boston Tea Party / Therese M. Shea.
Description: New York : Gareth Stevens Publishing, 2020. | Series: Team Time
  Machine: American Revolution | Includes index.
Identifiers: LCCN 2019011104| ISBN 9781538246825 (pbk.) | ISBN 9781538246849
  (library bound) | ISBN 9781538246832 (6 pack)
Subjects: LCSH: Boston Tea Party, Boston, Mass., 1773–Juvenile literature.
Classification: LCC E215.7 .S54 2020 | DDC 973.3/115–dc23
LC record available at https://lccn.loc.gov/2019011104

First Edition

Published in 2020 by
Gareth Stevens Publishing
111 East 14th Street, Suite 349
New York, NY 10003

Copyright © 2020 Gareth Stevens Publishing

Designer: Katelyn E. Reynolds
Editor: Therese Shea

Photo credits: Cover, p. 1 courtesy of the Library of Congress; cover, pp. 1–24 (series characters) Lorelyn Medina/ Shutterstock.com; cover, pp. 1–24 (time machine elements) Agor2012/Shutterstock.com; cover, pp. 1–24 (background texture) somen/Shutterstock.com; p. 5 Thiranun Kunatum/Shutterstock.com; p. 7 (main) The Print Collector/Print Collector/ Getty Images; p. 7 (map) pavalena/Shutterstock.com; p. 9 Hulton Archive/Getty Images; p. 11 f11photo/Shutterstock.com; p. 13 Interim Archives/Getty Images; p. 15 BPL (https://www.flickr.com/photos/24029425@N06)/Wikipedia.org; p. 17 Humanitiesweb.org/Cobalty~commonswiki/Wikipedia.org; p. 19 Bettmann/Getty Images; p. 21 Edward Gooch Collection/Getty Images; p. 23 Photo12/UIG via Getty Images; p. 25 (King George III) Kean Collection/Getty Images; pp. 25 (Governor Hutchinson), 27 (both), 29 MPI/Getty Images.

Printed in the United States of America

Some of the images in this book illustrate individuals who are models. The depictions do not imply actual situations or events.

CPSIA compliance information: Batch #CW20GS: For further information contact Gareth Stevens, New York, New York at 1-800-542-2595.

CONTENTS

WORDS IN THE GLOSSARY APPEAR IN **BOLD** TYPE THE FIRST TIME THEY ARE USED IN THE TEXT.

"I can't believe we have to do a project on the Boston Tea Party this weekend! I wanted to play basketball!" groaned Mia.

"Oh, it won't be that bad," said Sam. "It was just one night in 1773."

"There's actually a lot to learn," replied Ben. "We need to know who took part, why they did it, and its effects on the **American Revolution**.

"Let's head to the Team Time Machine library, and find out more!" suggested Mia.

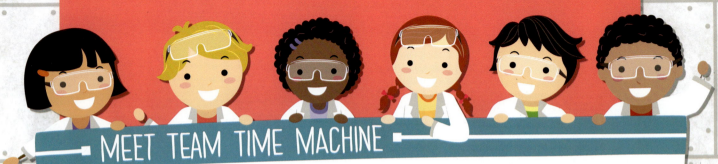

MEET TEAM TIME MACHINE

TEAM TIME MACHINE IS A GROUP OF FRIENDS WHO FOUND A TIME MACHINE ONE DAY IN A VERY ODD LIBRARY. THEY DISCOVERED THAT BOOKS FROM THE LIBRARY COULD POWER THE MACHINE AND TRANSPORT THEM TO DIFFERENT PLACES AND TIMES. IN THIS ADVENTURE, MIA, BEN, AND SAM TAKE PART IN THE BOSTON TEA PARTY!

THE TEAM TIME MACHINE LIBRARY IS FULL OF BOOKS ABOUT EVERY TIME AND PLACE YOU CAN THINK OF. TO TRAVEL TO ANOTHER TIME, YOU JUST NEED TO PLACE A BOOK IN THE MACHINE AND PULL THE HANDLE!

At the library, the friends found the section on the American Revolution. One of the books was called *The Boston Tea Party*.

"Get ready!" said Sam. He took the book from the shelf, placed it in a special slot in the time machine, and pulled the handle. The ground moved, and the room spun. The kids fell to the floor until the shaking stopped.

Ben got up and pulled open the library door. Outside was a busy street. But it wasn't a street from their time. "We're in **colonial** Boston!" he said.

WE FOUND OURSELVES IN BOSTON, MASSACHUSETTS—DECEMBER 16, 1773! THIS WAS THE DAY OF THE BOSTON TEA PARTY.

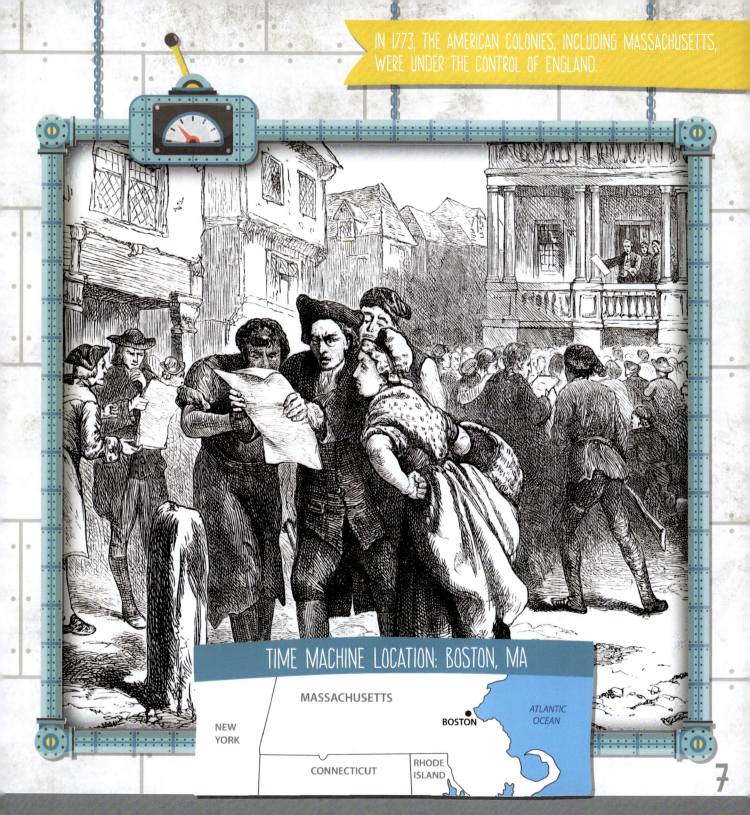

TIME MACHINE LOCATION: BOSTON, MA

NEW YORK

MASSACHUSETTS

BOSTON

ATLANTIC OCEAN

CONNECTICUT

RHODE ISLAND

The team quickly made a friend—a boy selling apples on the street. He called himself Johnny. He asked about their strange clothes.

"Um . . . we're from the West," explained Mia. That satisfied Johnny. He told them what was going on in Boston. Many colonists were angry about the taxes that England had been placing on British goods sent to the colonies. After many **protests**, most of the taxes had been repealed, or officially ended.

However, a tax on tea remained.

JOHNNY SAID THE AMERICAN COLONISTS WERE ESPECIALLY ANGRY ABOUT THE TAXES BECAUSE THEY HAD NO **REPRESENTATION** IN PARLIAMENT, THE BRITISH GOVERNMENT. NO ONE SPOKE UP FOR WHAT THE COLONISTS WANTED.

IN 1767, ENGLAND PASSED THE TOWNSHEND ACTS, WHICH PLACED TAXES ON BRITISH GOODS SHIPPED TO THE COLONIES. BY 1770, ALL THESE TAXES WERE REPEALED, EXCEPT FOR THE TEA TAX.

TAX·ON·TEA·

3ᵈ per lb

1773

Johnny invited them to a meeting at the Old South Meeting House. The kids stood in the back. Thousands were packed into the building.

"There's a shipment of tea in Boston Harbor," explained Johnny. "These colonists are deciding what to do with it."

Rather than pay the tax on the tea, the colonists voted to send the ships back. However, the royal Massachusetts governor, Thomas Hutchinson, refused to let the ships leave. He wanted the tea unloaded and the tax paid.

AMERICAN COLONISTS WERE ONLY ALLOWED TO BUY TEA FROM THE EAST INDIA COMPANY. COLONISTS LOVED TO DRINK TEA SO THE BRITISH GOVERNMENT THOUGHT THIS WAS A GOOD WAY TO RAISE MONEY.

THE OLD SOUTH MEETING HOUSE, WHERE THE MEETING ABOUT THE TEA IN THE HARBOR TOOK PLACE, IS STILL STANDING IN BOSTON TODAY.

CHAPTER 4: THE SONS OF LIBERTY

Outside the meeting house, Johnny told Mia, Ben, and Sam about a secret group fighting against British taxes. They were called the Sons of Liberty. Sometimes, they met under an elm tree in Hanover Square. They called it the Liberty Tree. Johnny pointed the way.

As the team approached Hanover Square, they saw some men under a large tree. The men were talking and looking over their shoulders. The kids may have looked like **spies**—the men ran off in different directions before they reached the tree!

THE SONS OF LIBERTY MOSTLY FOUGHT AGAINST THE BRITISH BY CREATING **PETITIONS** AGAINST TAXES, HOLDING MEETINGS, AND SPREADING POWERFUL **PROPAGANDA**.

"Well, that was a waste of time!" sighed Sam.

"Not if we follow them!" said Mia. The team trailed one of the men to see where he went. He ducked into a **tavern**—the Green Dragon. The kids went in, too. The man took a seat with a few other people, so the team sat nearby and listened.

"Hello, Samuel. What's the plan?" they heard someone say to the man.

"What can I get you, Mr. Adams?" asked a worker.

The team whispered, "It's Samuel Adams!"

MANY **PATRIOTS** WHO BECAME FAMOUS WERE SONS OF LIBERTY, SUCH AS SAMUEL ADAMS, PAUL REVERE, AND JOHN HANCOCK.

Green Dragon Tavern, Union Street.

Mia, Ben, and Sam tried to hear what Samuel Adams was telling the others at the table. The tavern was too loud to hear much. However, they did hear a few words, including "harbor," "**disguises**," and "natives." Then, Adams said, "Spread the word," and left in a hurry.

"He must be talking about the Boston Tea Party!" said Ben. "Let's go to the harbor and wait until night. We'll find a place to watch what happens."

BECAUSE SOME COLONISTS DIDN'T WANT TO SHOW SUPPORT FOR ENGLAND, THEY **SMUGGLED** TEA FROM OTHER COUNTRIES. SOME THINK SAMUEL ADAMS WAS A TEA SMUGGLER!

The kids got to Boston Harbor and hid behind some boxes. After running around all day, they found themselves getting cold in the December night.

"I don't think I can wait out here much longer," groaned Sam.

"Look!" hissed Mia.

A large group was heading toward them—more than 100 people! Did they see the team? No, they kept marching past. Some were dressed like Native Americans, but most didn't even bother. The kids watched as they climbed aboard three ships.

THERE WERE THREE EAST INDIA COMPANY SHIPS IN THE HARBOR. THEY WERE THE *DARTMOUTH*, THE *BEAVER*, AND THE *ELEANOR*.

"Let's get on one of those ships to get a closer look," suggested Mia. "It's dark and people are wearing disguises. They'll never notice!"

Sam and Ben agreed, and the team climbed aboard the *Dartmouth*. Mia was right. The colonists were so focused on destroying the tea that they didn't notice three more in the crowd, until . . .

"Hey, you three! Get working!" yelled one of the leaders. He handed Ben a small ax, and the team took turns chopping up wooden chests.

> MORE THAN 90,000 POUNDS (40,823 KG) OF TEA WERE THROWN INTO THE HARBOR. THAT AMOUNT WOULD COST ABOUT $1 MILLION TODAY!

"Ugh, revolution is tiring!" groaned Sam after several hours of work. Finally, the chopping stopped.

"Go home! And don't tell anyone what we did!" someone shouted. Everyone started to get off the ships and run in different directions.

"We'd better go, too!" said Ben.

The team was so tired. They didn't even have the strength to leave the harbor. They spotted a small ship with no one on board and fell fast asleep on the deck, under a sail.

ONLY ONE PERSON WAS ARRESTED FOR THE BOSTON TEA PARTY. HIS NAME WAS FRANCIS AKELEY. HE WOULD LATER DIE IN THE BATTLE OF BUNKER HILL DURING THE AMERICAN REVOLUTION.

IT TOOK 3 HOURS TO UNLOAD ALL THE TEA. IN ALL, 342 CHESTS WERE DUMPED IN THE WATER.

CHAPTER 7: COERCIVE CONSEQUENCES

Mia, Ben, and Sam woke to the sounds of screaming seagulls and shouts. They looked over the boat's edge. The events of the night had been discovered.

"Report this to Governor Hutchinson," they heard one British soldier bark at another. The team sneaked off the boat and found Johnny in the street. They told him what had happened.

"I heard! We all heard! It will take time for news to reach King George in England," said Johnny. "Will he be angry or will he give the colonies what we want?"

NOT EVERY PATRIOT APPROVED OF THE BOSTON TEA PARTY. GEORGE WASHINGTON AND BENJAMIN FRANKLIN WERE AGAINST IT. FRANKLIN WANTED TO PAY BACK THE EAST INDIA COMPANY HIMSELF!

KING GEORGE III IS OFTEN BLAMED FOR THE AMERICAN REVOLUTION. HOWEVER, GREAT BRITAIN'S PARLIAMENT HAD A LOT OF CONTROL OVER LAWS AND TAXES PASSED DOWN TO THE COLONIES.

KING GEORGE III

GOVERNOR HUTCHINSON

The team knew what happened next. They didn't need a time machine. In March 1774, laws called the Coercive Acts—or Intolerable Acts—were passed. They **punished** the colonists for the Boston Tea Party and other protests against British rule.

One law closed Boston Harbor until the colonists paid for the tea. A second put the British military in charge of Massachusetts. Another law protected, or guarded, British leaders blamed for crimes in the colonies. A fourth law allowed British soldiers to stay in colonists' homes.

"COERCIVE" MEANS "USING FORCE," AND "INTOLERABLE" MEANS "VERY UNPLEASANT." THE COLONISTS THOUGHT BOTH THESE WORDS WERE GOOD WORDS FOR THE NEW LAWS!

CHAPTER 8: WAR IS COMING

The American Revolution would begin in April 1775. But Team Time Machine had to get back—or go ahead—to its own time.

"If we did stay, we wouldn't have to do the Boston Tea Party project for school," suggested Mia.

"It'll be so easy now, Mia," said Sam. "C'mon, back to the time machine. We'll do the project and have time to play basketball."

"Sure!" said Ben. "Besides, it's getting dangerous around here!"

> THE TIME MACHINE TOOK US BACK TO OUR OWN TIME AFTER WE REMOVED THE BOSTON TEA PARTY BOOK. WE FINISHED OUR HISTORY PROJECT—AND GOT AN A!

To the King's Most Excellent Majesty.

Most Gracious Sovereign!

We your Majesty's faithful Subjects of the colonies of New-Hampshire, Massachusetts-Bay, Rhode-Island and Providence Plantations, Connecticut, New-York, New-Jersey, Pensylvania, the Counties of New-Castle, Kent and Sussex on Delaware, Maryland, Virginia, North-Carolina, and South-Carolina, in behalf of ourselves and the inhabitants of those colonies who have deputed us to represent them in General Congress, by this our humble petition, beg leave to lay our grievances before the throne.

A standing army has been kept in these colonies, ever since the conclusion of the late war, without the consent of our assemblies, and this army with a considerable naval armament has been employed to enforce the collection of taxes.

The Authority of the Commander in Chief, and under him, of the Brigadiers General has in time of peace, been rendered

GLOSSARY

American Revolution: the war in which the colonies won their freedom from England

colonial: having to do with colonies, which are lands under the control of another country

disguise: a false appearance

loyalist: someone who was on the side of the British during the American Revolution

patriot: someone who was on the side of the colonies during the American Revolution

petition: a written request signed by many people asking the government to take an action

propaganda: ideas or statements that are often false or overstated and are spread to help a cause

protest: an event at which a group objects to an idea, an act, or a way of doing something

punish: to make someone suffer for wrongdoing

representation: a person or group that speaks or acts for or in support of another person or group

smuggle: to move something from one country into another illegally and secretly

spy: a person who tries secretly to get knowledge about a group for another group

tavern: a place where people eat and drink

FOR MORE INFORMATION

BOOKS

Landau, Elaine. *The Boston Tea Party: Would You Join the Revolution?* Berkeley Heights, NJ: Enslow Elementary, 2015.

Marciniak, Kristin. *12 Incredible Facts About the Boston Tea Party.* North Mankato, MN: 12-Story Library, 2016.

Russo, Kristin J. *Viewpoints on the Boston Tea Party.* Ann Arbor, MI: Cherry Lake Publishing, 2019.

WEBSITES

American Revolution: Sons of Liberty
www.ducksters.com/history/american_revolution/sons_of_liberty.php
Find out more about this secret organization.

Boston Tea Party
www.history.com/topics/american-revolution/boston-tea-party
Read more about why the Boston Tea Party happened and the effects it had on the American Revolution.

INDEX